555 Sticker Fun
Football

Licensed exclusively to Imagine That Publishing Ltd
Tide Mill Way, Woodbridge, Suffolk, IP12 1AP, UK
www.imaginethat.com

0 2 4 6 8 9 7 5 3 1
Manufactured in China

A very windy game!

It is very windy at today's qualifying football match. Add stickers of players chasing the ball to stop it from being blown away. Add spare balls, too.

5

Playing in the rain

It has been raining for days! This qualifying match is turning into a very soggy game. Add teams of muddy players trying to avoid the puddles.

The hottest match ever

It is the hottest day of the year and the teams are gasping for their half-time drink. Add thirsty footballers trying to keep going until the whistle blows.

Go girls, go!

This girls' qualifying match has gone into extra time. The crowd is very excited! Use stickers to fill the pitch with players doing their best to win.

2 : 2

At the airport

Spain have made it through to the final tournament. Add the players to this airport scene and all the luggage they need for their trip.

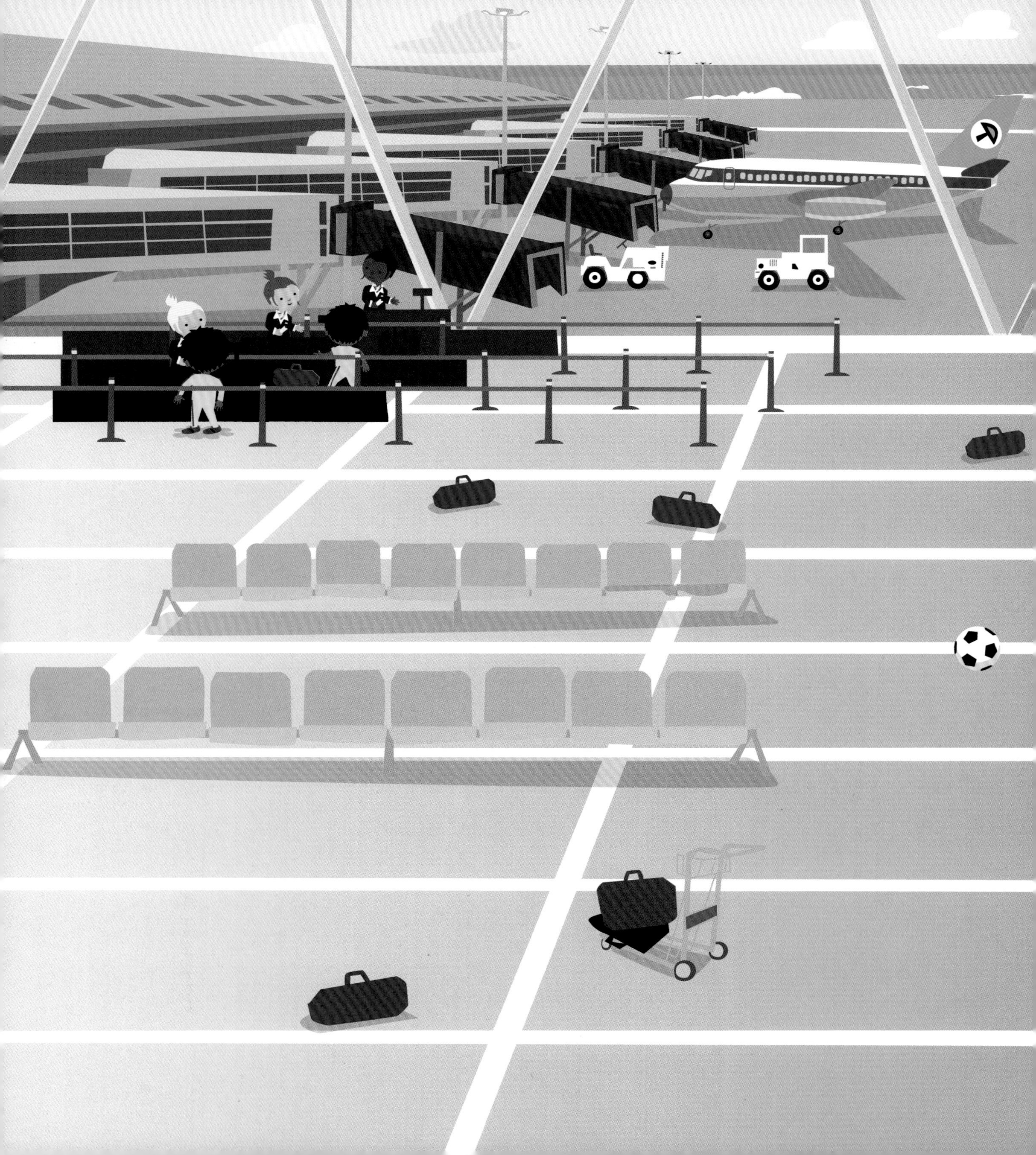

20 – 51

On the tour bus

The German team have arrived for the tournament. Fill the tour bus with stickers of tired players looking forward to a good night's sleep.

At the training camp

The Portuguese players have arrived at their training camp. The facilities are fantastic! Use the stickers to fill the scene with exploring teammates and some more vehicles.

Tip-top fitness

At Argentina's training camp, the coach is making his team work very hard. Add stickers of exercising players, so the manager can check for tip-top fitness.

Tour bus drama

The Italian tour bus has a flat tyre. Add the players, manager and driver trying to fix the problem, so they can get to their game on time. Add some other vehicles too.

Traffic jam!

There are thousands of people travelling to the stadium. Use stickers to pack the roads with vehicles of all kinds.

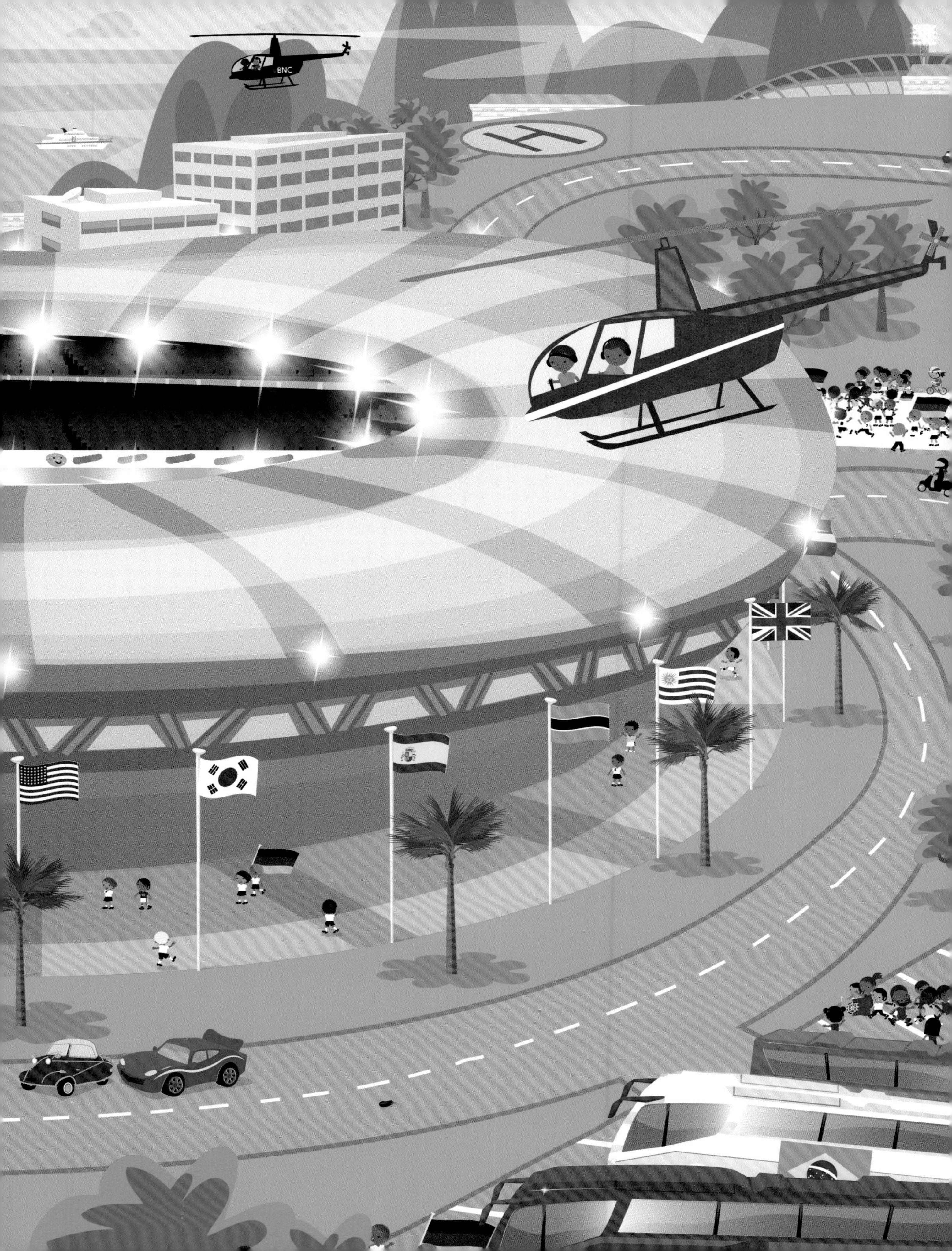
BNC

In the spotlight

The stadium lights have gone out at this evening match, but the clever caretaker has found some spares. Now you can add players in the spotlights.

Caught on camera

A television cameraman has got too close to the action. He has been knocked out! Add stickers of concerned footballers, checking that he is okay.

In the commentary box

The commentator has a great view of this quarter-final match. At the moment, Spain are losing to Brazil. Fill the pitch with players using all their skill to beat their rivals.

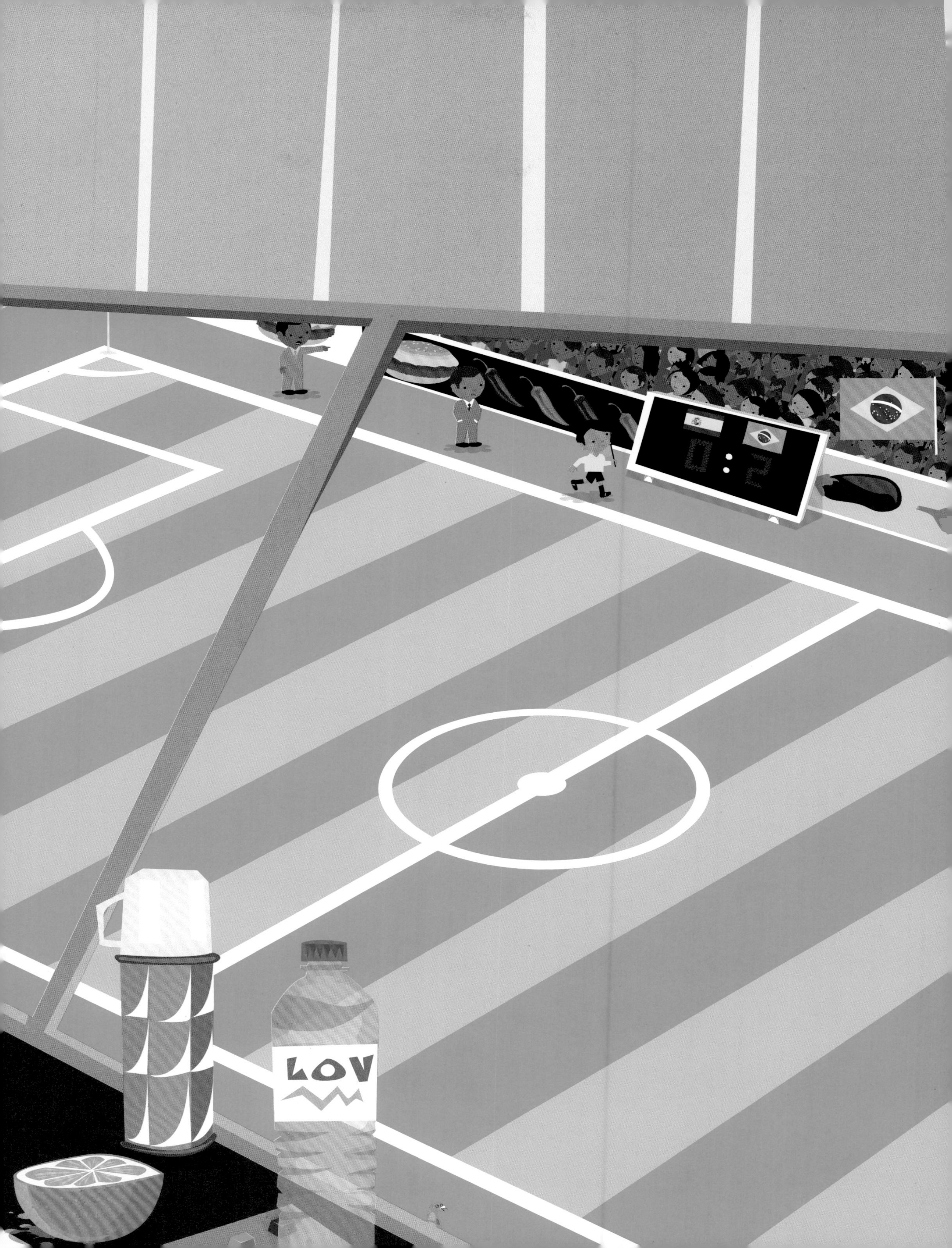
0 : 2
LOV

Half-time

The Spanish coach is giving his team a half-time talk. Add tired players to the benches. They will feel better after something to eat and drink.

7
8
9
11
12

Super supporters

The girls' teams have finished their matches. They have come to watch Italy play France. Fill the VIP box with excited girls cheering the teams on.

Bring on the stretcher!

It is the Germany-Argentina quarter-final. The German captain has injured himself in a brave tackle. Add the medical team with a stretcher to help him out.

Penalty shoot-out

It is time for a penalty shoot-out in the Portugal-England quarter-final. Use the stickers to position all the players, ready for the moment of truth.

4 : 4

Excited fans!

The tournament semi-finals are about to start. Fill the streets with excited fans waving flags in celebration. Can you work out which teams will play?

VBNC

The first semi-final

Italy, Germany, Spain and Portugal have made it to the semi-finals. Choose stickers of the two teams you want to play in this match. Add them to the pitch for an action-packed game.

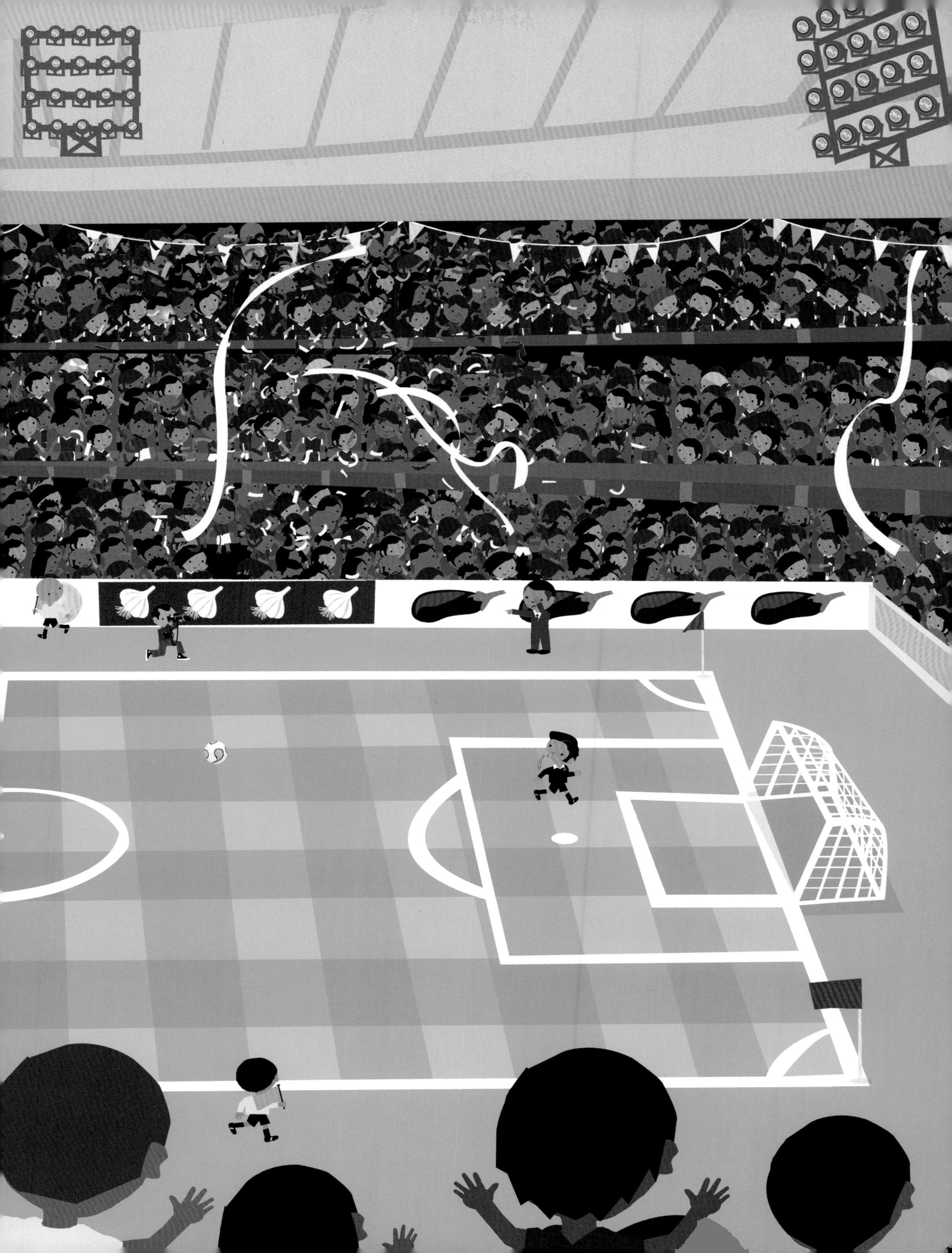

The second semi-final

It is time for the second semi-final. Choose the two teams you want to play in this match. Add them to the pitch for some midfield drama.

Preparing the pitch

It is the night before the grand final. Add stickers of groundsmen preparing the pitch. Then add more stadium staff checking that everything is working.

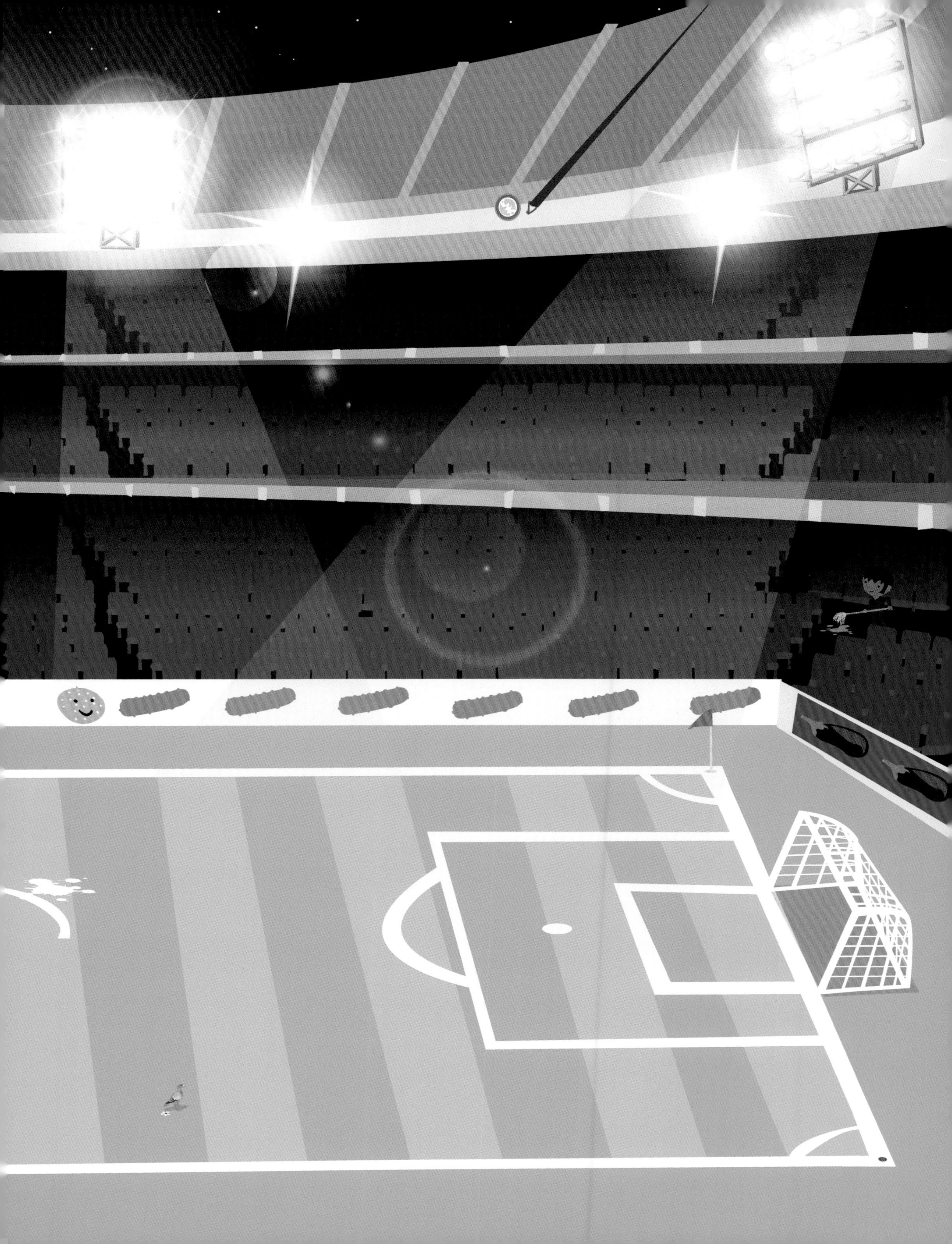

The big interview

Everyone is excited at the pre-match interview. Add reporters, photographers and camera teams. Then add a line-up of international players predicting who will win.

The grand final

It is the day of the grand final. Decide which teams you want to compete for the cup. Then use the stickers to create a game to remember.

The winners!

Who has won the grand final? You can decide. Select the stickers of your winning team and add them to the podium. It's time to celebrate!

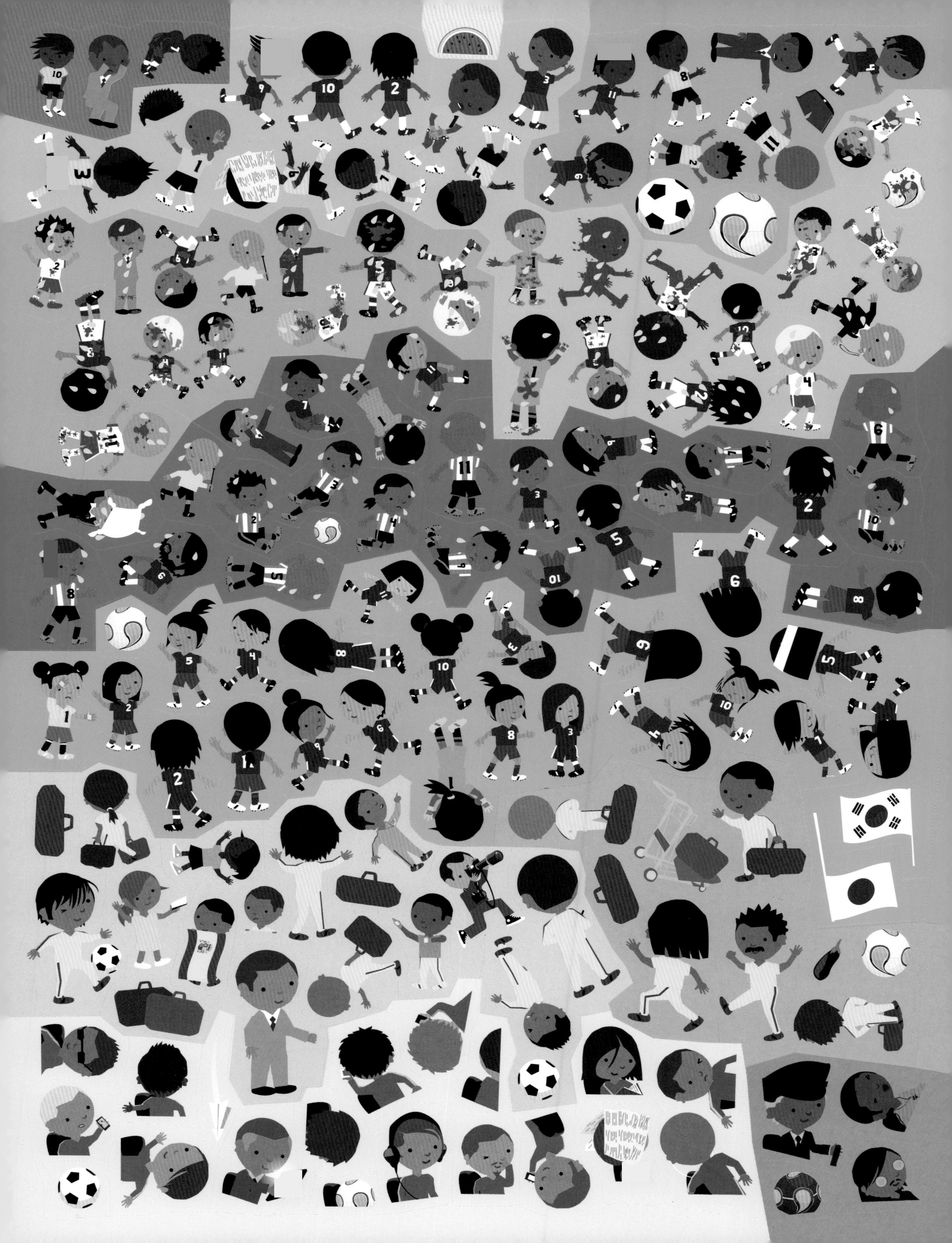

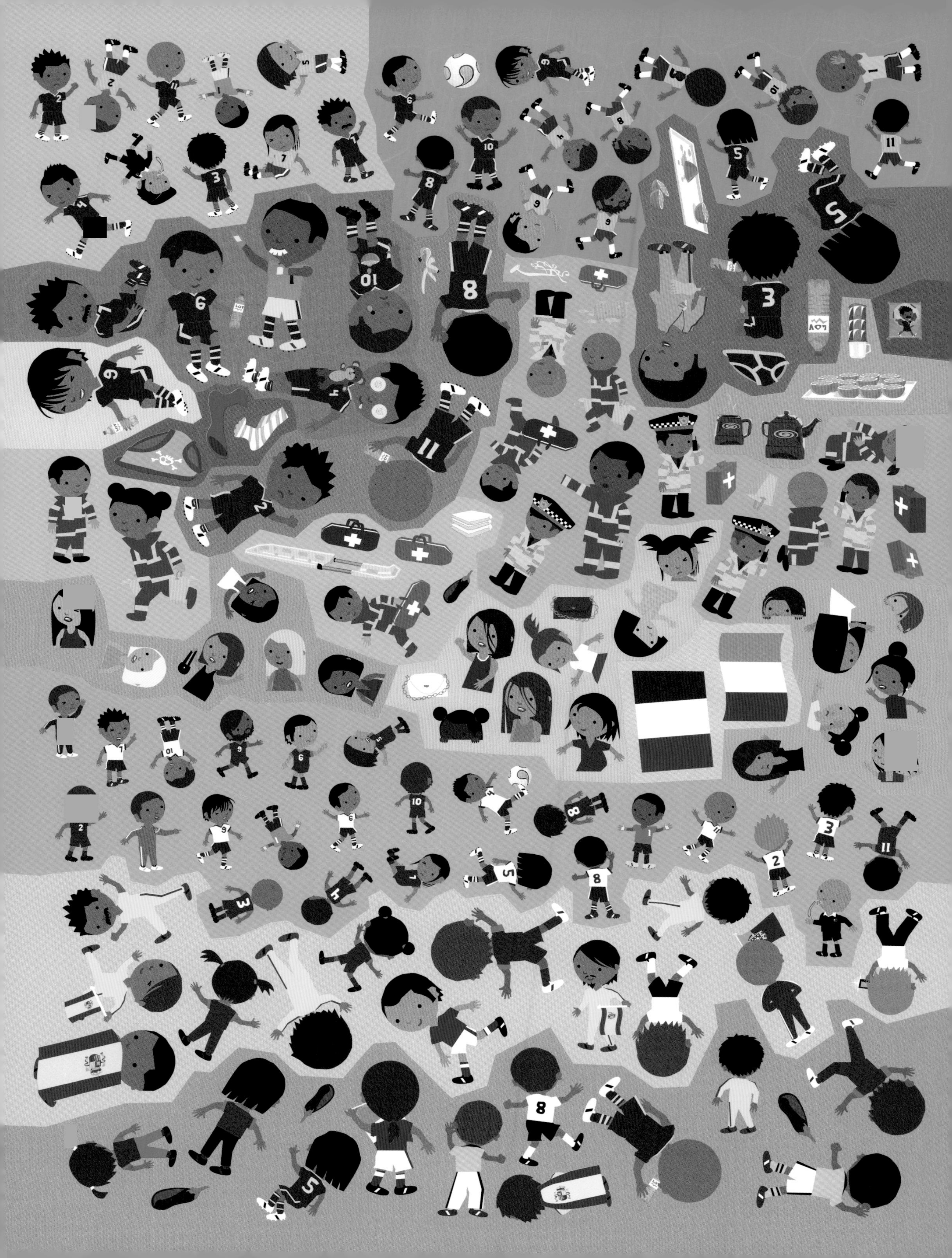